Action Sports

Mountain Biking

California School for the De
Riverside

Bill Gutman

Illustrated with photographs
by Shawn Frederick

Reading consultant:
John Manning, Professor of Reading
University of Minnesota

Capstone Press

MINNEAPOLIS

Printed in the United States of America.

Capstone Press • 2440 Fernbrook Lane • Minneapolis, MN 55447

Editorial Director   John Coughlan
Managing Editor   John Martin
Copy Editor   Gil Chandler

Library of Congress Cataloging-in-Publication Data

Gutman, Bill.
    Mountain biking / by Bill Gutman.
        p.   cm. -- (Action sports)
    Includes bibliographical references (p.   ) and index.
    ISBN 1-56065-234-9
    1. All terrain cycling--Juvenile literature. [1. All terrain cycling.]   I. Title.   II. Series
    GV1056.G88   1995
    796.6--dc20   94-31769
                                                        CIP
                                                        AC

ISBN: 1-56065-234-9

99 98 97 96 95   8 7 6 5 4 3 2 1

Table of Contents

Chapter 1
Mountain Biking

For many people, mountain biking is just for fun. They like to get out and enjoy the scenery and the weather. At the same time, they bike to stay in shape.

Other mountain bikers ride to explore new places or to challenge themselves on rough terrain.

For others, mountain biking is a demanding sport. These riders seek the toughest roads and races. They like the challenge, or maybe they just want to win. Whatever the reason, racers try to get the most out of their bodies and their bikes.

Mountain biking is one of the fastest growing sports in the world. Mountain bikes are getting better and can go almost anywhere. Police and messengers use them in the cities. In the country, they can climb mountains, cross streams, go through mud, and scramble over rocks.

Mountain biking is many things to many people. It's fun and healthful, and it may be just the sport for you.

Chapter 2
How Mountain Biking Started

The first mountain bikes came from a much smaller bike called the **BMX** (which stands for "bicycle motocross") bike. BMX bikes were designed for very young riders, and became popular in the early 1970s. Rugged **frames** and thick tires made them ideal for doing tricks, jumping, racing, and riding over rough terrain.

The first mountain bikes came from BMX bikes.

9

Kids could do things on these bikes that they couldn't do on thin-wheeled, 10-speed bikes. The BMX bike, however, had just one **gear**. It was hard to pedal up hills or ride long distances, but it could easily go down rough hillsides. Soon, BMX biking was very popular in California.

Many adults who watched BMXers wanted to ride like them. But 10-speed bikes couldn't take the pounding, and BMX bikes were too small for adult riders.

Mountain bikes can handle all kinds of rough terrain. This rider pedals over an abandoned railroad track.

Chapter 3
The First Mountain Bikes

A bike builder named Joe Breeze set out to solve this problem. He used the basic BMX design to make an adult bike. He gave this bike a strong frame, powerful hand brakes, additional gears for hills, and a flat handlebar. The new bike also had thick, rugged tires.

The new bikes didn't catch on right away. They were so different from the 10-speeds that people thought they looked funny. But riders soon learned that the bikes could go places their 10-speeds could never go. By the mid-

1980s, the bikes were selling fast. By 1990, the boom in mountain bikes was underway.

A new cycling association started: the National Off-Road Bicycle Association (NORBA). Mountain bikers all across the country joined.

When You Get Your Own Bike

A new mountain bike can be very costly. Inexpensive bikes sell for as little as $100 to $150. But high-quality bikes cost much more–about $600 or $700. The top-of-the-line bikes cost $3,000 or more. Special equipment and accessories can raise the price even higher.

New mountain bikers should buy the best bikes they can afford. If you have a limited budget, you can get an inexpensive bike to start. But if you like the sport you'll want to start saving for a better one.

The Frame

The most important part of a mountain bike is the frame. It must be rugged, yet lightweight. The first frames were made of steel.

Later, builders switched to aluminum, a lighter metal. Some frames are now made from a titanium alloy. Alloys combine different metals and other components.

A mountain-bike frame is longer than that of a 10-speed. There is also more space between the frame and the wheels. This allows the mountain bike to handle mud and other kinds of rough terrain.

The Fork and the Tires

The front **fork** of a mountain bike is thicker than a 10-speed fork. In recent years, many new kinds of forks have been invented. Most good mountain bikes now have **suspension forks** in the front. They're almost like the shock absorbers on a car. They give a smoother ride and cause less stress on the rest of the frame.

Mountain-bike tires usually have a heavy tread with large bumps called "**knobbies**." Many of these tires are more than two inches (three centimeters) wide–twice the width of a 10-speed tire. Yet thick tires perform just as well as 10-speed tires, even on paved roads. The wheel rims are usually made of aluminum or another tough, lightweight alloy. They are wider than the rims of 10-speeds and smaller in diameter.

Gears, Pedals, and Brakes

Like 10-speeds, mountain bikes use derailing gears. Good bikes can have 15 to 18 gears or more, with three **chainwheels** and six back **sprockets**. This gives the rider gears for any kind of road or trail.

The pedals have large metal teeth for a strong foot grip. Most do not have toe clips, but these may be added.

Mountain bikers often ride up and down very steep trails. Their bikes must have good brakes. Mountain bikes use a cantilever brake system, which is different from the caliper brakes used on 10-speeds. Cantilever brakes have extra thick cables and are better at slowing down the mountain bike's thick tires.

The **saddle** on the mountain bike is also different. It's wider and has more padding than

17

The many gears on a mountain bike allow the rider to tackle steep hills and rough terrain.

a 10-speed racing seat. A new system includes a seat and a post that move back and forth. This gives the rider better balance. It also makes it easier to shift gears.

Mountain bikes come in many sizes. Make sure yours is the right size for you. When you sit on the bike, you should be able to touch the ground with the balls of your feet. If you can't, or if you have to really strain to reach, the bike is too large. If your feet are flat on the ground, or your knees are bent, the bike is too small.

You should also be able to reach the handlebars comfortably. Your arms should be almost fully extended, and your hands and shoulders relaxed. You won't feel comfortable if the frame is too large or too small.

Chapter 4

Safety and Maintenance

New mountain bikers must be aware of safety. On the road, bikers should always watch out for cars. Keep your eyes and ears open, and always signal and look before making a turn. When riding off-road, watch for other riders. They may be traveling at higher speeds, or they may not see you. Use common sense and don't take chances.

Protective Gear

It's important for all bikers to wear helmets. Climbing hills and crossing rough terrain can be dangerous. All bikers fall at some time, and a head injury can be serious. A fiberglass or plastic helmet with foam padding inside will give you excellent protection.

If you fall, long-sleeve shirts and long pants will protect you from scrapes and bruises. In hot weather, you'll probably want to wear shorts and a T-shirt or tank top. With these, you should also wear knee and elbow pads.

There are special shoes for racing, and riding gloves will protect your hands and give you a better grip. A helmet is a must. Wear the rest according to the weather and the kind of riding you will be doing. Remember: safety first!

Maintenance

Maintenance is a big part of bike safety. The worst enemies of mountain bikes are dirt and moisture. Mud can clog up the **derailleur** and sprockets. Use a brush to scrape it off. A hose and water will get off the loose mud.

After you wash the bike, be sure to dry it. Moisture can cause rust. You should also lubricate the gears and brakes with a light oil.

All bikers take falls—but the best riders are prepared with good safety equipment.

Safety and Maintenance Checklist

1. Check and tighten any loose bolts on your brake levers, shifter levers, stem, handlebar, and bar ends.

2. Check the weld area of the stem for cracks.

3. Check for cracks on both sides of the stem.

4. Check the outer casings of the brake and shifter cables for cracking or kinks. Make sure the cables are not frayed or blocked.

5. Check the ends of the derailleur cables. Make sure they're not frayed.

6. Check your tires for worn and torn treads. Also check for cuts and tears in the tire.

7. Check the welds on the frame for signs of cracking.

8. Check the cage fixing bolts on platform pedals and the small nuts and bolts on clipless pedals. Also, check the pedal cleats for wear.

If you take good care of your bike, it will last a long time and be safe to ride. You can learn more about your equipment from repair manuals, from people who run bike shops, and from experienced riders.

Chapter 5

Mountain Biking Basics

The first thing to learn about mountain biking is how to use the many gears. The middle gears are best for riding on smooth, flat surfaces. The high gears are for downhill riding and for **tailwinds**.

Low gears are used for riding up hills. They are also used when a strong **headwind** is blowing in your face. Low gears are good for riding through mud and for getting a quick start.

Two levers on the handlebars shift the gears. They are usually moved with the thumbs. Each lever operates a derailleur. One derailleur controls the chainwheels. The other controls the back sprockets.

Changing Gears

You must be pedaling the bicycle when you change gears. Otherwise, the chain cannot move onto the next chainwheel or sprocket.

You cannot shift both derailleurs at the same time. If you do that, the chain may fall off. It is also not a good idea to shift more than one gear at a time.

Shifting takes practice. Go slowly at first. Soon you'll know by the terrain and by the feel of the bike which gears you should be using.

Rough terrain may force you to carry your bike. To do this, just loop your right arm (or left, if you prefer) under the crossbar that runs from the seat to the front stem. Bring the crossbar up to your shoulder and grab the handlebars with your right hand. Your shoulder does the lifting and carrying.

Getting On the Bike

There is a right way to mount the bike. With the bike in a low gear, stand on its left side, with the left pedal to the front and halfway up the chainwheel. Grab the handlebars with both hands and place your left foot on the left pedal. Swing your right leg up and over the seat, and push down on the left pedal. As the bike begins to move, put your right foot on the right pedal. You're off!

Braking

On most bikes, the left hand controls the front brake, the right hand the rear brake. The front brake is used to make normal stops. (That's because about 70 percent of your braking power comes from the front brake.)

When braking hard, move your weight back and keep low in the seat. This will keep the rear wheel from coming off the ground. When you're riding downhill, use both brakes.

Learn how your brakes work under different conditions. Wet, muddy terrain causes a loss of power in the rear brake.

A mountain bike can take you off the beaten paths and away from the crowd.

Maximum Braking Point

Learn your maximum braking point. That is the fastest stop you can make without going into a skid. This takes practice, especially on different downhill grades. You can also control your brakes better by riding off the seat. Extend your arms, but keep your elbows bent. This keeps the weight off the front wheel.

Always keep the braking rims clean. If dirt from the pads builds up on the rims, it can cause poor braking. Clean the rims with steel wool, and your brakes will work better.

Chapter 6

Advanced Riding Techniques

The "Wheelie"

The first advanced skill a mountain biker should learn is the **"wheelie."** This means getting the front wheel into the air. Wheelies help you hop over obstacles, one of the big challenges of mountain biking.

There are several ways to do a wheelie. If you have a bike with standard forks, you

Some spots will force you to carry the bike, no matter how good a rider you are.

should lean back in the seat while you pick up speed. Before you reach the obstacle, pull up and back on the handlebars. This should lift the front wheel off the ground. This takes practice. You don't want the wheel to come up too high.

As the front wheel clears the obstacle, lift off the seat and move forward. This allows the back wheel to clear the obstacle.

Suspension forks let you do a different kind of wheelie. When you reach the obstacle, push down on the forks, drop your hips, and push your knees forward. As you release the forks and shift your weight upward, the front wheel will come up.

Wheelies are an important part of mountain biking. A new rider should practice them every day, until he's confident when approaching any obstacle.

Getting Off the Ground

To clear a small obstacle or a ditch, you may want to get both ends of the bike off the ground at the same time. First, do the wheelie. Then

push forward hard on the handlebars. This will make the bike see-saw. The front will drop and the back will come up.

At high speed, you can also bring your body up and forward. It's easier if you have toe clips and can pull up with your feet.

If you are leaping a wide ditch, keep pedaling hard. If you don't quite clear the ditch, pedaling might bring the rear wheel up and over the edge.

Downhill Riding

When riding downhill, you should keep your feet out of the toe clips. Stand slightly, squeeze the seat with your thighs, and keep the cranks level, with your stronger foot forward. Your upper body should be balanced between the front and back.

Always look as far ahead as you can on a downhill trail. The earlier you can spot a hazard, the better you'll be able to handle it. Be extra careful on a twisting course where you can't see beyond the next bend.

Rocky trails are no obstacle for a skilled mountain biker.

Climbing

Climbing hills can be a tough challenge.
Don't take on more than you can handle.
When you pedal up a hill for the first time, go
slowly. Don't try to charge up. If you get
really tired, stop and rest.

To be a real hill climber, you should have a
bike that has the right gear ratio. A 24-tooth

A pair of riders speeds downhill on a tandem mountain bike.

front chainwheel with a 32-tooth rear is a good climber. So is a 22-tooth front and a 30-tooth rear. A 20-tooth front works well with a 28-tooth rear.

Good Traction

You also need good **traction**. Good traction is when you're pedaling as hard as you can and the rear wheel isn't spinning. Get a good feel for the wheel. This is the key to climbing.

Most low-gear climbing is done sitting down. On short, steep climbs it is sometimes better to stand. One trick is to shift to the middle chainwheel as you get off the seat. If you don't stand on a steep climb, move closer to the handlebar and drop your head and shoulders.

To get better traction, stand and lift the front wheel over large rocks and ledges. Then pull the back wheel onto the obstacle and use it to get more traction. Always look up the trail to see where you'll have the best traction.

Singletrack Riding

Many bikers love to ride **singletrack**–a narrow trail just wide enough for a single bike. It may be a horse trail, or even a trail created just for bikers. Singletrack can be difficult and sometimes dangerous. It takes an experienced rider to handle everything that comes up on these trails.

Here are a few tips for singletrackers. If you come to a banked turn, always come up on the outside, or high side, of the bank. Lean into the turn. The outside edge of the bank will help, and you won't have to turn the handlebars as much.

If you reach a sandy spot, be careful on turns. The more you turn the handlebar, the more the wheel will plow the sand forward and resist the turn. Instead, just lean the bike in the direction of the turn. This is the best way to turn in sand.

Beginning singletrackers should use toe clips. The clips will keep your feet firmly on the pedals through all the leaning and turning.

When singletracking, always look ahead as much as you can. If there is a rider in front of you, try to see past him. If it's a friend, have him tell you if he sees a hazard up ahead. If the trail becomes very rough or dangerous, stop. There's nothing wrong with carrying your bike past a dangerous spot. In fact, carrying is often the smart thing to do.

There are many different things you can do on a mountain bike. And there are many challenges and dangers. Always make sure you're skilled enough to meet the challenge.

Chapter 7

Mountain Bike Racing

There are several kinds of races for mountain bikers. Some bikers travel all over the country to race against the clock and against each other.

Circular Obstacle Racing

Circular obstacle course racing is similar to motocross racing. The racers must circle the track a set number of times. The first across the finish line is the winner. Racers have to go fast, avoid collisions, and take the jumps and turns as fast as they can.

Uphill-Downhill Racing

Most uphill-downhill races are timed events. The riders pedal to the top of a steep hill, then race down a marked trail. It takes both uphill and downhill skills to do well in these events.

Cross-Country and Challenge Races

In cross-country races and challenge races, bikers race from the starting line to the finish line, choosing their own routes over rough terrain.

There are separate races for men and women and for different age groups. If you're ready to race, contact a mountain-biking club or one of the national organizations.

Glossary

BMX–a small, rugged bike for kids. BMX stands for "bicycle motocross."

chainwheels–the large, toothed rings near the front of the bike, on which the chain rides. The chainwheels are turned by the pedals.

derailleur–the mechanism controlled by the rider which moves the chain from one sprocket and chainwheel to another.

forks–the part of the frame that holds the front tire

frame–the main body of the mountain bike, constructed of lightweight, tubular steel, aluminum, titanium or various combinations of metals

gears–the various combinations of chainwheels and sprockets upon which the chain rides. The gears control the power ratio transmitted from the pedals to the wheels.

headwind–a wind that is blowing against the rider

knobbies–the knob-like projections on a mountain-bike tire

saddle–the seat on a mountain bike

singletrack–a trail wide enough for only one bike at a time. Singletracks are favorites among many experienced riders.

sprocket–the group of smaller toothed wheels that carry the chain at the rear of the bike

suspension forks–forks on high quality mountain bikes that have a set of shock absorbers built in

tailwind–a wind blowing at the rider's back

traction–the ability of a tire to grip the road or trail without skidding or spinning

wheelie–a maneuver in which the front wheel of the bike is lifted off the ground to go over an obstacle on the trail

To Learn More

Abramoski, Dwain. *Mountain Bikes.* New York: Franklin Watts, 1990.

Allen, Bob. *Mountain Biking.* Minneapolis, MN: Lerner Publications, 1992.

Coombs, Charles. *All-Terrain Bicycling.* New York: Holt, 1987.

Lafferty, Peter. *Pedal Power: The History of Bicycles.* New York: Franklin Watts, 1990.

Wood, Tim. *Mountain Biking.* New York: Franklin Watts, 1989.

You can read articles about mountain biking in two magazines: *Bicycling* and *Mountain Biking*.

Some Useful Addresses

National Off-Road Bicycle Association
NORBA
P.O. Box 5513
Mill Valley, CA 94942

League of American Wheelmen (LAW)
P.O. Box 988
Baltimore, MD 21203

Bikecentennial
P.O. Box 8303
Missoula, MT 59807

Canadian Cycling Association/Association cycliste canadienne
1600 James Naismith Drive, Suite 810
Gloucester, ON K1B 5N4

International Mountain Bicycling Association
Route 2, Box 3
Bishop, CA 93514

Index